W9-BFR-481

The new Solar System

The Sun

Robin Birch

CHELSEA CLUBHOUSE

An Imprint of Chelsea House Publishers

This edition published in 2008 in the United States of America by Chelsea Clubhouse, a division of Chelsea House Publishers.

Chelsea Clubhouse
An imprint of Chelsea House Publishers
132 West 31st Street
New York, NY 10001

Chelsea Clubhouse books are available at special discounts when purchased in bulk quantities for businesses, associations, institutions, or sales promotions. Please call our Special Sales Department in New York at (212) 967-8800 or (800) 322-8755.

You can find Chelsea Clubhouse on the World Wide Web at: http://www.chelseahouse.com

First published in 2004 by
MACMILLAN EDUCATION AUSTRALIA PTY LTD
15–19 Claremont Street, South Yarra, 3141

Visit our Web site at www.macmillan.com.au or go directly to www.macmillanlibrary.com.au

Associated companies and representatives throughout the world.

Library of Congress Cataloging-in-Publication Data

Birch, Robin.
    The sun / Robin Birch. — 2nd. ed.
    p. cm. — (The new solar system)
    Includes index.
    ISBN 978-1-60413-205-2
    1. Sun—Juvenile literature. I. Title.
    QB521.5.B57 2008
    523.7—dc22

                                    2007051542

Edited by Anna Fern
Text and cover design by Cristina Neri, Canary Graphic Design
Photo research by Legend Images
Illustrations by Melissa Webb, Noisypics

Printed in the United States of America

Acknowledgements
The author and publisher are grateful to the following for permission to reproduce copyright material:

Cover photograph of the Sun courtesy of Photodisc.

Michael Jensen/Auscape, p. 22; Tom Till/Auscape, p. 5 (bottom); Australian Picture Library/Corbis, p. 4; Wendy Carlos & Jay M. Pasachoff/SOHO, p. 11; Corbis Digital Stock, p. 23 (top); Digital Vision, pp. 5 (top), 6, 7, 13, 25; ESA/NASA/SOHO, p. 29; Calvin J. Hamilton, p. 9; MarieLochman/Lochman Transparencies, p. 23 (bottom); NASA/MIX, p. 27 (bottom); Photodisc, pp. 12, 14, 15; Photolibrary.com/SPL, pp. 8, 10, 19, 21, 26, 27 (top), 28.

Background and border images, including view of the Sun, courtesy of Photodisc.

While every care has been taken to trace and acknowledge copyright, the publisher offers their apologies for any accidental infringement where copyright has proved untraceable. Where the attempt has been unsuccessful, the publisher welcomes information that would redress the situation.

Please note
At the time of printing, the Internet addresses appearing in this book were correct. Owing to the dynamic nature of the Internet, however, we cannot guarantee that all these addresses will remain correct.

Contents

Glossary words

When you see a word printed in bold, **like this**, you can look up its meaning in the glossary on page 31.

The Sun

People have always seen the Sun in the sky. **Ancient** peoples worshipped the Sun, which brought light and warmth for their crops to grow.

The ancient Greeks worshipped the Sun god Helios. They believed that Helios drove the Sun across the sky in a horse-drawn chariot.

▲ This is the symbol for the Sun.

▶ Helios

Later, the ancient Romans adopted Helios as their Sun god and called him "Apollo." The ancient Chinese people's Sun god travelled across the sky in a chariot drawn by dragons. The ancient Egyptians had four Sun gods. The most important was Ra, the god of the midday Sun.

Until the 1500s, the Mayan, Incan, and Aztecan peoples of Central and South America all built temples for Sun worship. The temples lined up with the rising and setting Sun, which helped the people follow the seasons.

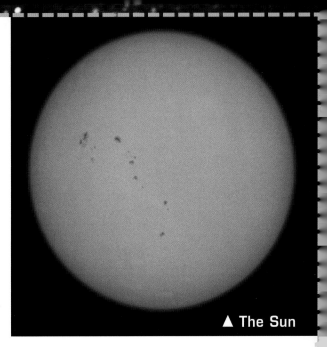

▲ The Sun

Ancient English people erected stone circles that helped them follow the Sun across the seasons. One example is Stonehenge, which was built between 3,000 and 2,000 BC.

In ancient times, people used to believe that the Sun circled around Earth. It was only about 400 years ago that people understood that Earth circles around the Sun. Today, people study the Sun with **telescopes**, and send **space probes** to gather information about it.

▼ Stonehenge

The Sun is a Star

The Sun is a star. It is a huge ball of very hot, glowing **gas**, like other stars.

Sun's Formation

The Sun formed in a huge cloud of hydrogen gas. The gas swirled around and formed a tight ball, and heated up. When the gas ball reached a temperature of 18 million degrees Fahrenheit (10 million degrees Celsius), nuclear fusion began inside it.

In nuclear fusion, hydrogen particles join together to make particles of the substance helium. When they do this, huge amounts of heat and light energy are given off.

When nuclear fusion began in the ball of gas, the ball became a star, the Sun. This happened about 4,600 million years ago.

> The ancient Romans called the Sun "*Sol*." Today the official name for the Sun is "Solaris."

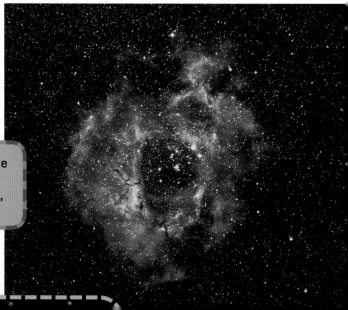

► This gas cloud has young stars in it.

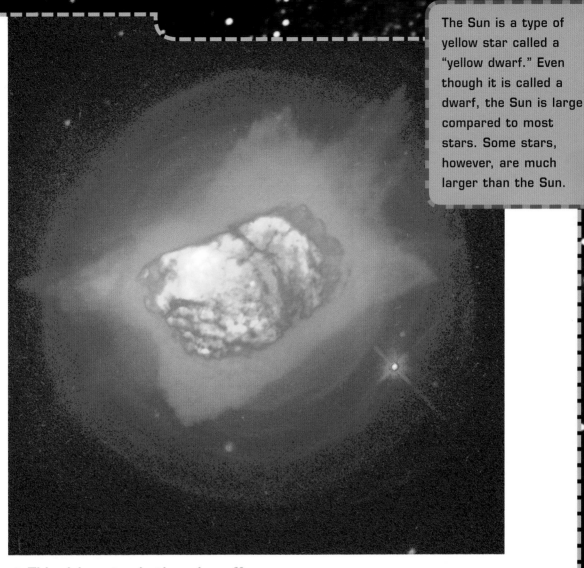

▲ This dying star is throwing off gas.

In about 5,000 million years from now, the Sun will run out of hydrogen gas. Then nuclear fusion in the **core** will stop, and a different type of nuclear fusion will spread into the outer layers. The Sun will expand and become a red color. It will then be what is called a "red giant" star. The Sun will probably be so large at this time that it will swallow up Earth.

The red giant Sun will eventually collapse. As it collapses, it will throw off gas. The Sun's core will become an object called a "white dwarf."

The Solar System

The Sun formed at the center of a huge cloud of gas. Many other bodies were formed at the same time and they revolve around the Sun. The Sun and these bodies together are called the solar system.

The solar system has eight planets. Mercury, Venus, Earth, and Mars are made of rock. They are the smallest planets, and are closest to the Sun. Jupiter, Saturn, Uranus, and Neptune are made mainly of gas and liquid. They are the largest planets and are farthest from the Sun.

The solar system also has dwarf planets. The first three bodies to be called dwarf planets were Ceres, Pluto, and Eris. Ceres is an asteroid. Pluto and Eris are known as **trans-Neptunian objects**.

A planet is a body that:
- orbits the Sun
- is nearly round in shape
- has cleared the area around its orbit (its **gravity** is strong enough)

A dwarf planet is a body that:
- orbits the Sun
- is nearly round in shape
- has not cleared the area around its orbit
- is not a **moon**

▲ The solar system

Planet	Average distance from Sun	
Mercury	35,960,000 miles	(57,910,000 kilometers)
Venus	67,190,000 miles	(108,200,000 kilometers)
Earth	92,900,000 miles	(149,600,000 kilometers)
Mars	141,550,000 miles	(227,940,000 kilometers)
Jupiter	483,340,000 miles	(778,330,000 kilometers)
Saturn	887,660,000 miles	(1,429,400,000 kilometers)
Uranus	1,782,880,000 miles	(2,870,990,000 kilometers)
Neptune	2,796,000,000 miles	(4,504,000,000 kilometers)

The name "solar system" comes from the word "Sol," the Latin name for the Sun.

▶ The eight planets are Mercury, Venus, Earth, Mars, Jupiter, Saturn, Uranus, and Neptune.

The solar system is about 4,600 million years old.

There are also many small solar system bodies in the solar system. These include asteroids, comets, trans-Neptunian objects, and other small bodies which have not been called dwarf planets.

Asteroids are made of rock. Most of them, including dwarf planet Ceres, orbit the Sun in a path called the asteroid belt. The asteroid belt lies between the orbits of Mars and Jupiter. Comets are made mainly of ice and rock. When their orbits bring them close to the Sun, comets grow a tail. Trans-Neptunian objects are icy, and orbit the Sun farther out on average than Neptune.

On the Sun

The huge, hot Sun is the closest star to Earth. It orbits the center of the **galaxy**, speeding through space at 137 miles (220 kilometers) every second.

Size and Structure

The Sun is 863,000 miles (1,390,000 kilometers) in **diameter**. It is about 109 times wider than Earth.

The center of the Sun, called the core, has a temperature of 27 million degrees Fahrenheit (15 million degrees Celsius). The core is where nuclear fusion takes place. In the nuclear fusion, hydrogen is converted into helium. Energy is released from this process, which makes the Sun's heat and light.

Outside the Sun's core is the radiative zone and then the convective zone. The energy released in the core takes one million years to pass through these layers and reach the surface.

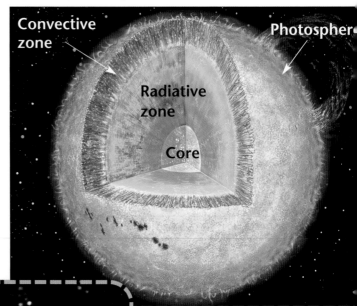

▶ Parts of the Sun

Convective zone

Photospher

Radiative zone

Core

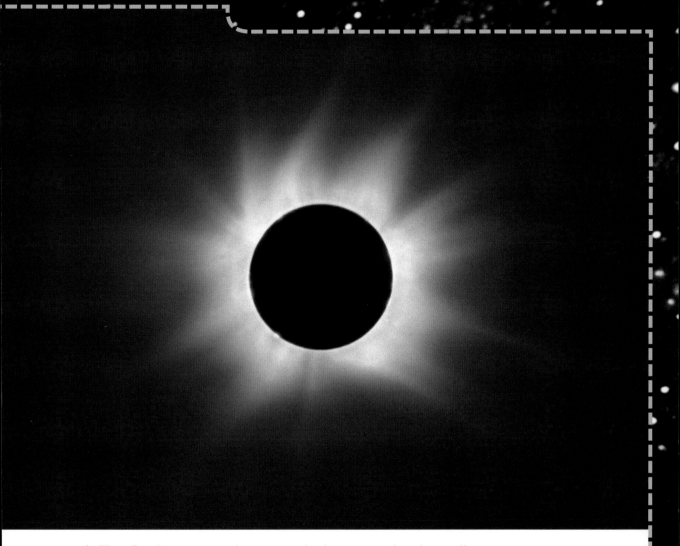

▲ The Sun's corona shows up during a total solar eclipse.

The outside surface of the Sun is called the photosphere. Around the photosphere is a thin layer of gas known as the chromosphere. Outside the chromosphere is another layer of gas called the corona. The corona extends a long way out from the Sun.

The Sun is about 75 percent hydrogen and 25 percent helium. However, the hydrogen is gradually being converted to helium. Over time, there will be less and less hydrogen, and more and more helium.

Photosphere

The surface layer of the Sun, called the photosphere, is about 300 miles (500 kilometers) thick. It has a mottled appearance, like boiling water. The temperature of the photosphere is 9,900 degrees Fahrenheit (5,500 degrees Celsius). The energy produced in the Sun's core is released from the photosphere as heat and light.

The photosphere **rotates** at different speeds in different places. At the Sun's **equator**, the photosphere rotates once every 25.4 days. At the **poles**, the photosphere takes up to 36 days to rotate once. The Sun can rotate at different speeds because it is made of gas.

"Photosphere" means "sphere of light."

▼ The surface of the Sun has a mottled appearance.

Sunspots

Sunspots are spots on the Sun's photosphere. They appear dark because they are cooler than the gas around them. Their temperature is about 6,300 degrees Fahrenheit (3,500 degrees Celsius). Sunspots are usually found in groups. Their number builds up over a period of 11 years, then drops. The size of sunspots can range from a few hundred miles across to larger than Earth.

Solar Flares

Solar flares are eruptions of gas and energy from parts of the photosphere that have sunspots. There are more solar flares when there are more sunspots.

Solar Prominences

Solar prominences are huge solar flares which leap long distances from the Sun.

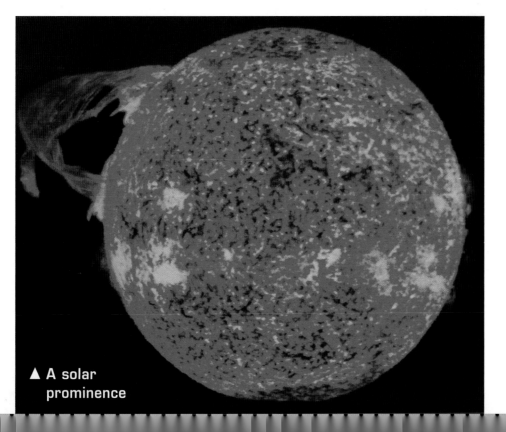

▲ A solar prominence

Chromosphere

The chromosphere is a layer of hot gas which is just above the photosphere. It is about 1,600 miles (2,500 kilometers) thick. The lower part of the chromosphere is cooler, then its temperature rises to about 18,000 degrees Fahrenheit (10,000 degrees Celsius) towards the top.

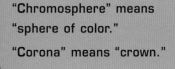

"Chromosphere" means "sphere of color."

"Corona" means "crown."

◀ The chromosphere can be seen in this picture of a total solar eclipse.

Corona

The Sun's corona is an area of very thin gas which extends millions of miles from the Sun. It reaches temperatures of millions of degrees and is heated by **magnetic** energy from the Sun. It cannot be heated by the Sun's surface, as the surface is much cooler. The corona can be seen in pictures of a total solar eclipse. The corona becomes the solar wind, as it passes through the solar system.

The solar wind blows comet tails away from the Sun.

Solar Wind

The solar wind is the name given to the part of the Sun's corona which stretches to the edge of the solar system. It is a stream of **charged** particles which spreads out from the Sun in all directions. It usually takes about a week for the particles to travel from the Sun to Earth.

When the charged particles in the solar wind reach Earth, some get trapped in Earth's **magnetic field**. Sometimes they fall towards the ground near the North and South poles. They make curtains of light in the sky, called "auroras," or the northern or southern lights. When the solar wind blows more strongly, it can affect electricity supplies and radio communications.

15

Sun and Earth

The Sun's energy supports life on Earth. The Sun is also the main force behind Earth's seasons and weather.

Day and Night

Earth rotates on its **axis** once every 24 hours. Because of this, we see the Sun rise in the east, pass across the sky, and set in the west. The Sun appears to move, but it is really Earth that is moving.

From most of the Northern **Hemisphere**, the Sun is seen passing through the southern sky. From most of the Southern Hemisphere, the Sun is seen passing through the northern sky.

Never look straight at the Sun, even with sunglasses. It will burn your eyes if you look at it.

Sun

Axis

Day

Night

▲ Where the Sun shines onto Earth, it is daytime.

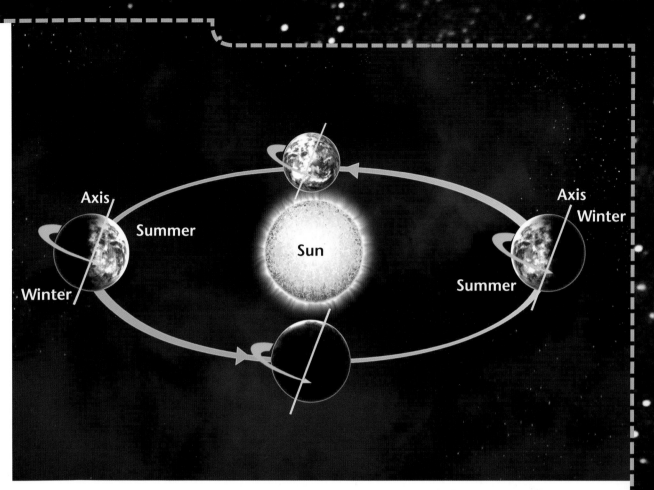

Seasons

Earth revolves around the Sun in one year. Earth's axis is tilted, which causes seasons on Earth.

When the Northern Hemisphere is tilted toward the Sun, it has summer. The Sun rises north of east, and sets north of west. When the Northern Hemisphere is tilted away from the Sun, it has winter. The Sun rises south of east, and sets south of west.

When the Southern Hemisphere is tilted toward the Sun, it has summer. The Sun rises south of east, and sets south of west. When the Southern Hemisphere is tilted away from the Sun, it has winter. The Sun rises north of east, and sets north of west.

Rays from the Sun

The Sun **radiates** different kinds of rays. The rays we can see are called visible light. The other rays are gamma rays, X rays, ultraviolet rays, infrared rays, and radio waves.

Earth's atmosphere stops dangerous gamma rays, X rays, and ultraviolet rays from reaching the ground. Visible light rays light up Earth, and infrared rays heat Earth.

▼ Earth's atmosphere stops some of the Sun's rays.

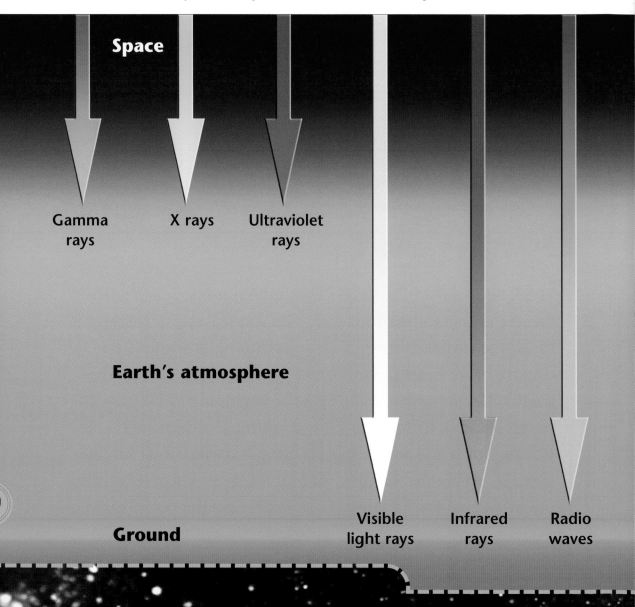

Space

Gamma rays

X rays

Ultraviolet rays

Earth's atmosphere

Ground

Visible light rays

Infrared rays

Radio waves

▲ The Sun's spectrum, seen through a spectrometer

We see the Sun's spectrum when there is a rainbow. The sunlight is broken up by the water drops in the sky.

The Color of Sunlight

Sunlight is a white color. When it shines though a prism, such as a piece of cut glass, the white light breaks up into rainbow colors, called a spectrum.

An instrument for collecting a spectrum is called a spectrometer. A spectrum made from sunlight by a spectrometer looks like a piece of a rainbow with thin black lines across it. The lines are caused by different substances on the outside of the Sun, such as iron and sodium. **Astronomers** have discovered a lot of detailed information about the Sun by studying its spectrum.

Sun Energy

Sunlight is used to make electricity. Solar cells collect sun energy and make electricity for many different uses, from operating toys, to powering cars and homes.

Heat from the Sun is collected to heat water for use in homes and swimming pools. This is known as solar heating.

Heat from the Sun drives the weather on Earth. The Sun heats up water so that it **evaporates**. The water collects in clouds, then falls as rain. The Sun also heats up air, which produces winds.

▼ Solar cells on the roof of a solar-powered vehicle

▲ Animals eat plants grown in sunlight.

Energy for Living Things

The Sun gives living things the energy they need. Plants use sunlight to make their food in a process called "photosynthesis." Without sunlight, plants cannot make their food. Animals eat plants to get their energy. In this way, animals also rely on sunlight for their energy.

Plants and animals need water to live. The Sun is warm enough to melt ice, so that there is water, but not so hot that the water dries up. The Sun provides warmth for living things. It is not too hot and not too cold.

▶ Reptiles are cold-blooded, and need heat from the Sun to warm up.

23

Solar Eclipses

Once a month, the Moon passes between Earth and the Sun. Usually the Sun and the Moon do not line up exactly, so the Moon does not block out the Sun's light. However, sometimes the Moon does line up exactly with the Sun, and does block the Sun's light. This is called a solar eclipse, or an eclipse of the Sun.

The Sun and the Moon are almost exactly the same size in the sky. This is because the Sun is 400 times wider than the Moon, but it is 400 times farther away. When the Moon covers the Sun exactly, the sky goes dark. This is called a total eclipse. If the Moon only partly covers the Sun, it is called a partial eclipse, and the sky stays bright.

▼ During a solar eclipse, the Moon's shadow darkens part of Earth.

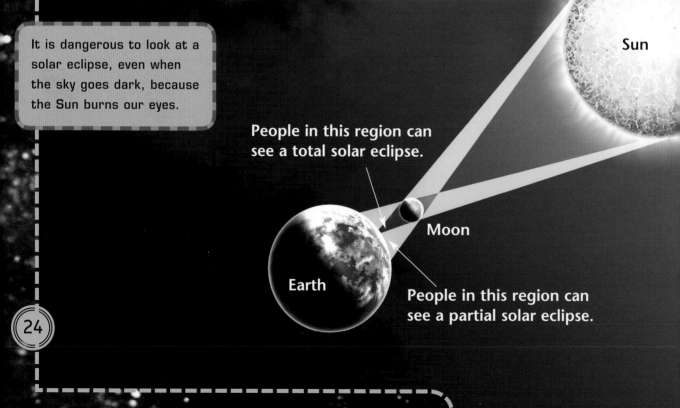

It is dangerous to look at a solar eclipse, even when the sky goes dark, because the Sun burns our eyes.

People in this region can see a total solar eclipse.

Sun

Moon

Earth

People in this region can see a partial solar eclipse.

▼ A total solar eclipse

When the sky goes dark during a total solar eclipse, the stars shine, the temperature goes down and birds settle down on the trees.

Total Eclipses

A total solar eclipse can last for up to 8 minutes, but usually lasts for only about 2 minutes. The Sun's corona shows up as glowing light around the Moon. The pink chromosphere also shows up around the edge of the Moon, along with pink solar prominences leaping from the Sun's surface.

When there is a total solar eclipse, it only occurs along a long but narrow path on Earth. Many people travel long distances to observe a total solar eclipse. Partial solar eclipses occur over a much wider area.

Studying the Sun

People have been studying the Sun since ancient times. Today, space probes and solar telescopes help us to learn about the Sun.

The Sun was first studied by the ancient Greeks and Romans, who mostly believed that Earth was the center of the **universe**, and the Sun circled around it. A Greek astronomer, Aristarchus, who was born in 310 BCE, realized the Sun was much bigger than the Moon, and farther away. He also thought the planets circled around the Sun. Other astronomers at the time did not believe him.

In 1543, Nicolaus Copernicus again suggested that Earth circled the Sun. He was not believed until telescopes gave new information, about 100 years later. Today, we know that eight planets orbit the Sun.

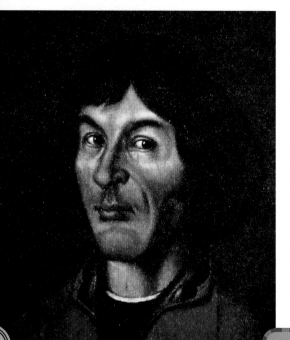

▲ Nicolaus Copernicus

Nicolaus Copernicus was a Polish astronomer, born in 1473. He was a church official and a doctor.

Solar Telescopes

Astronomers use special telescopes, called solar telescopes, to study the Sun. Other telescopes would burn our eyes very quickly if we looked at the Sun through them. Solar telescopes have a mirror at the top which turns to face the Sun. The mirror reflects the Sun's light down a tube, where it is shone onto a screen, where it can be looked at and photographed. This is a safe way of observing the Sun.

▲ A solar telescope

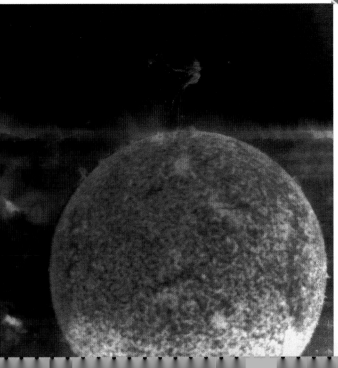

▼ This picture was taken by *Skylab* astronauts in 1973.

One way of taking good pictures of the Sun is to photograph it from space. *Skylab* was a space station which orbited Earth in 1973 and 1974. It had a crew of three **astronauts** who took more than 150,000 pictures of the Sun, using solar telescopes.

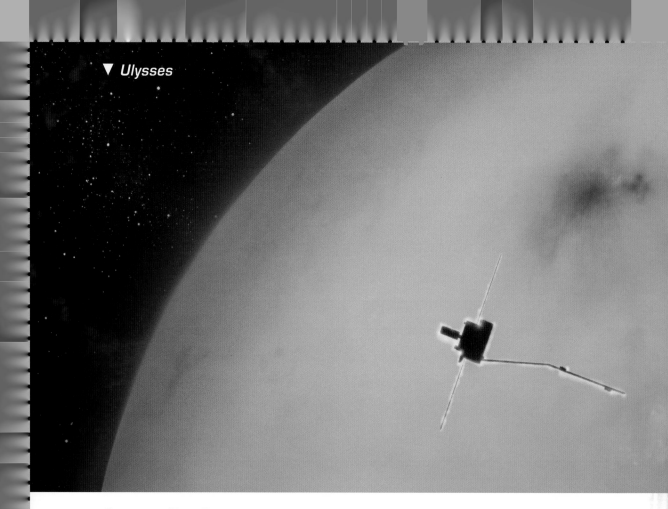

▼ *Ulysses*

Space Probes

Many space probes have studied the Sun. They detect X rays and ultraviolet rays coming from the Sun, as well as light rays.

The *Ulysses* probe was launched in 1990. Its aim is to observe the north and south poles of the Sun, and to detect what may be in space high above them. *Ulysses* discovered holes in the corona above the poles.

The space probe *SOHO* (short for *"Solar and Heliospheric Observatory"*) was launched in 1995. Its goal is to help astronomers work out the structure inside the Sun, and to watch how the Sun's surface rises and falls. Astronomers also want to use *SOHO* to study the Sun's corona and the solar wind, by collecting ultraviolet light.

Questions about the Sun

There is still a lot to learn about the Sun, and astronomers will continue to send space probes to study it. One day, astronomers hope to find out the answers to questions such as these:

- Why is the Sun's corona so much hotter than the photosphere? It would seem impossible that the corona could get hotter higher up.
- What is the exact cause of sunspots?
- What would be found in space above and below the poles of the Sun? Earth revolves around the Sun's equator, and we really only know about our part of space.

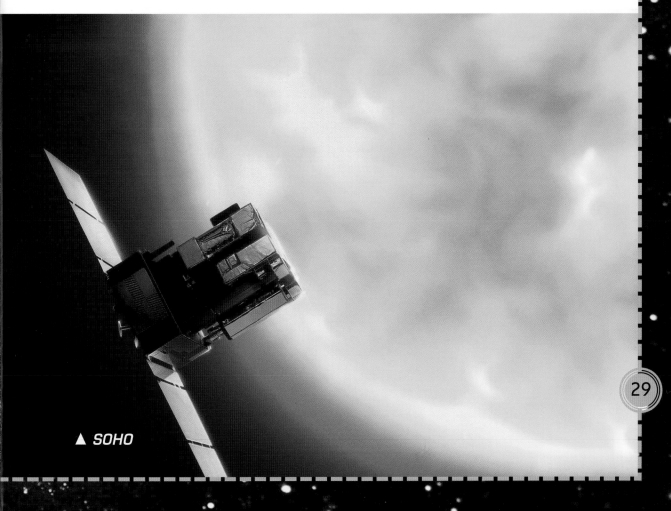

▲ SOHO

Sun Fact Summary

Diameter	863,000 miles (1,390,000 kilometers)
Mass	333,000 times Earth's mass
Density	1.41 times the density of water
Gravity	27.9 times Earth's gravity
Temperature (at surface)	9,900 degrees Fahrenheit (5,500 degrees Celsius)
Rotation on axis	25.4 Earth days (at equator)
Revolution around galaxy	220 million years
Planets	8

Web Sites

www.astro.uva.nl/demo/sun/kaft.htm
The Sun

www.nineplanets.org/
The eight planets—a tour of the solar system

www.enchantedlearning.com
Enchanted Learning Web site—click on "Astronomy"

stardate.org
Stargazing with the University of Texas McDonald Observatory

Glossary

ancient lived thousands of years ago

astronauts people who travel in space

astronomers people who study stars, planets, and other bodies in space

atmosphere a layer of gas around a large body in space

axis an imaginary line through the middle of an object, from top to bottom

charged carrying electric energy

core the center, or middle part of a solar system body

density a measure of how heavy something is for its size

diameter the distance across

equator an imaginary line around the middle of a globe

evaporates changes from a liquid into a gas

galaxy a huge group of many millions of stars (the solar system is in the Milky Way galaxy)

gas a substance in which the particles are far apart, not solid or liquid

gravity a force which pulls one body towards another body

hemisphere half of a globe

magnetic has the force of a magnet, to attract other similar objects

magnetic field an area where magnetism occurs

mass a measure of how much substance is in something

moons natural bodies which circle around planets or other solar system bodies

orbit *noun* the path a body takes when it moves around another body; *verb* to travel on a path around another body

poles the top and bottom of a globe

radiates gives off something

revolve travel around another body

rotates spins

space probes unmanned spacecraft

telescopes instruments for making faraway objects look bigger and more detailed

trans-Neptunian objects small solar system bodies which orbit the Sun farther out than Neptune, on average

universe all of space

Index